KNOWING

Also by Mark Cox

Readiness: Prose Poems
Sorrow Bread: Poems 1984-2015
Natural Causes: Poems (Pitt Poetry Series)
Thirty-Seven Years from the Stone
Smoulder
Barbells of the Gods

KNOWING

POEMS

MARK COX

Press 53

Winston-Salem

Press 53, LLC
PO Box 30314
Winston-Salem, NC 27130

First Edition

Author photo by Adrianne Mathiowetz

Library of Congress Control Number
2024931880

ISBN 978-1-950413-79-9

For my children,
Austin, Rachel and Keith

Contents

I.
THE DANCE

II.
SHELTER

III.
WHAT IS THIS THEN BETWEEN US

IV.
WONDER BREAD

I.

THE DANCE

Music Box

For Ralph Angel

Everything's just peachy, comes the world report: all clear. We are not pirouetting on the tip of time's scalpel; we are not screwing deeper into the ground's veneer. It is just the fleeting dance we do until the delicate box closes, having learned now to bow before hurting ourselves.

Today is Thursday once again and the man next door is off to get his mail. He will wander back reading, as is his wont to do, his wizened leashed dachshund dog sniffing at the leaves. The breeze passes over our shrubs and still they stand. A wary sparrow peers from them but we shouldn't call it hiding.

Yes, we have learned how to brace for the brief plunge toward otherness. We have learned to keep our eyes open to the dark, even if it doesn't matter. We see most vividly what cannot be seen, and this is always the case.

In the caves of our past, flames flickered on the rough walls. Fear grew there beyond reason and all sense of proportion. Our shadows have always been bigger than we are, the house lights shining up as they do, not down.

It would make sense to be offered a tune now. Something simple and genuine, a tale of longing fulfilled. Something to do with a childhood nightlight, a mother's cool palm. Whatever it is, it will have to be a memory wound long ago.

Such a blessing might be broadcast from just about anywhere. We receive it on this bureau with no clue wherefrom it issues, which ancient satellite or lofty transmission tower. On and off like a warning beacon, the message beams. Once all is said, one has no choice but to choose. Call it grace, call it wonder, just, as they say, keep it calling.

The Dance

For Jack Myers

Jack, if you are looking for me, my room's at the back, in the far depths of the Boston Sheraton, its locked window overlooking a shaft of brick and exhaust covers, a maintenance court squared by four distinct wings. Here, the shaded wind is trapped, less sure. Split off from upper currents, it vacillates and veers, a dizzying indecision embodied in the snow it wields—urgent, whirling cyclones of it— swept from rooftop heaps by happenstance. Watching this recalls the shoreline at Winthrop, and how we set some ashes just beyond the water's edge, where the tide would rise and claim you. You had become so very small. It seemed more just than trusting fickle winds. And it felt wrong to cast you on the waters, to see you drown in a dark your poems forestalled. Instead, the welling deep came almost tenderly, tugging first at the edges of the mound, then seeping inward to dampen the core, to draw you not so much out into the ocean as down into the rich coast's shore, a peace below the current's roiling reach. There, on that beach, it was as if some timeless otherness proffered a passage home. . . . No, Jackie, nothing quite so trite or grand—it was more a sweaty, steadfast partner, guiding you toward a crowded floor and music we can enter, but never understand.

The Remnants

Herewith, the liberation of roses, the bombardment of freesia in darkness, one smear of candlelight marring night sky. This is how the infinite gets made again. One lover says this, the other says that. The cat pads the garden crouching low. I don't know about you, but I often doubt our own existence. It is all too vaporous to be true. But then the alternative is what? I have re-drawn my archways. I have converted my cathedral. We make of history what we can, the stuff of life, the leavings of others, the mere sketches to which we are reduced—charcoal on paper, wisps of smoke and hair. Throughout it all, night's insects offer vague accompaniment. It is the quiet's fault. There is so much air here, it hurts. This is where the pastoral gets t-boned by an errant thought. Shattered, it survives in shards of the lens itself. Myself, I fear the dotted line traversing maps in old movies, the implied arrow. I have forgotten more than I remember. The shadow of my life grows larger than my life. But I digress before I begin. May I assume you have ventured here for counsel? Each couple's method will be unique but always you must first lie in each other's arms and let the exit haunt you. I will count backward from ten. Begin whenever you want.

Hand

(Auguste Rodin, c. 1886)

Predisposition renders
what I think I know,
but whether this hand
is poised to grasp

or has just let go,
matters much less
than what extends away.

I can only guess
what Rodin meant to say.

Denied full wrist and forearm,
no fixed body
is fully implicit; no
one lone form cast free
from our confusion of forms.

Is it a sign meant to hush and warn?
Or is it a jazz player's hold
without his horn?

Is it someone elderly,
needing help to stand,
or an explorer sinking
into cruel quicksand?

So many ways to *take* this hand.

To ask who it is, then,
is to reveal who you are;
to expose set dualities
and psychic scars.

Brother, father,
sister, mother—
is it ever truly
one or the other?

It lures with temptation
and extends salvation.
It marks duration
and signals affirmation.
It shows closed borders
of self, no doubt, *and*
a newfound persona thrusting out.

Nothing, really, stays withheld
or without.

What is proffered is intimacy.
What is granted is promise.
What is projected, ultimately,
in this charged void of space,

are our own fragile bodies
and their fleeting embrace.

Sunday

The children have been playing on the floor, Sunday trousers scuffed and dirtied at the knee. Their only wish is just ten minutes more, but coffee hour is over, presently. Parents now coerce them into vans, having had their gossip, gab and politics; it's time for exodus to weekend plans—clean grills, close pools, blow leaves, and rake up sticks. Surplus donut holes are rolled back in their box; they'll be at the nursing home by afternoon. All doors are barred and every window's locked; the gravel lot appears a grid of runes. The shut sanctuary's air is cool and dim, its stained-glass smears the pews as if with blood. The rough cross above the altar beareth Him, writhing and beseeching unto God.

Docent

I too resist nagging and dislike being led, so I really can't blame you for lagging behind, it is a compelling painting and a cool floor, but there are limits to this life and you have reached mine, so please, kiddo, get up and rejoin the rest, if you glean nothing else from religious art today, let it be that one does what's expected or is liberally punished—look again at that cross, does it look like a family outing to you? And those saints, bouquets of arrows in their hearts, you don't want to end up like them, do you, it is no picnic being stoned down to size—the other kids, they know we'll miss lunch at this rate, we still have the Pre-Raphaelites and Early Moderns to go—what do you say, son, up off your knees, there'll be another chance for penance in the next wing—hell, at least tag along and pretend to listen, I know I can drone on, but I studied art at Princeton, I passed the docent exam in record time, I know 14 different ways to say "don't touch that," including Swahili and Portuguese—c'mon kid, it is my livelihood you are toying with, I have to move three groups a day, I get a bonus for every head I herd to the gift shop, so, up you go, those tootsies can't hurt that much, and what more can you possibly divine that you didn't know from Ben Hur—Ok, ok have it your way, we'll be in antiquities a few minutes should you change your mind, after that, you can catch up in the 18th century—please tell me that isn't blood on your hands, I am starting to get worried about you, do not take this stigmata thing too much to heart, it is just a museum, after all, so on second thought, up and away now, there's no time like the present, we are detouring to Greek statuary, come and see! done right the human form is pretty racy. Rilke never got over how alive and wet marble looks, it really does seem they've been in a sauna for centuries—that luminous sheen, that far-off look in their eyes, can you spell ecstasy, can you say rapture? I thought so, I thought that might do it, so what do you say, hop to, up and at 'em, the nice guard here will help get you safely back behind the cordon. . . .

True North

Looking back for a low point marking the worst of my insobriety, it might be that signal moment I put out my cigarette in the holy water font of St. Paul's Catholic church, right in front of the priest, I might add, who was too stunned to reach in and remove the soggy stub, but who looked at me with such fervent scorn I could feel his ire through the entire service.

What was I to do? The water had been so *still* and the font had really seemed so much like an ashtray and it *was* by an entrance—it all made complete sense to me. This was the seventies, of course, which is why I was even smoking inside a church at all (that made complete sense to everyone then), and I was young, and as I implied before, would have been imbibing at the time. We were there for a wedding, and I was a Protestant guest, an outsider unschooled in the mysteries of the Roman Catholic order, naïve about its rituals and rules. I probably kneeled when I wasn't supposed to; God knows I may have stretched out on the pew, for all I remember. I suspect we had been celebrating the nuptials some days in advance, I suspect I was standing before God with the matchbook of a strip club in my pocket and had probably bathed with a washcloth at best, dressing hastily in the back of a van with carpet on its walls. Now surely, my soul was bound for hell. There was no sweet-talking my way out of this one.

Even thinking of it now I shudder a bit; I can hear the woman behind me gasp as that red-hot Camel straight hissed against the surface of the water. I can see it floating there, turning a little from side to side, like a compass needle coming to true north, the paper's glue starting to give way, flecks of tobacco bobbing at the uncharred end. Bless me father, for I have sinned, big time. I am sorry about the scene I caused. I am sorry about the shame. I am not, however, sorry about that bridesmaid, in fact, my only regret is that I don't remember more of her, but then that is the tragedy of youth, you can't have it forever, not even in memory, especially when you've slaughtered as many brain cells as me, but there's no use crying over spilt, well, bourbon. . .

I am a model citizen now. I go to bed early. I'm asleep by ten o'clock. I don't recall my dreams and my days follow one upon another like the pickets of a snow-white fence. What have I learned? There is a hair's difference between self-love and self-harm; both being self-importance and delusion. Ironically, I had to prove how unimportant I truly was before I could be happy being trivial. I needed to stand before God as a complete buffoon to make peace with my imperfectness. I had an ego I really should have been licensed to carry.

And what about that font? Should I have recognized what it was right off? Should I have guessed it was something sacred? At the very least, I should have plucked that butt post haste, secreting it in my pocket while slinking into the sanctuary, but I was as shocked as everyone else and ultimately, shamed and clueless, I just shambled to the back pews.

The bride and groom lasted 16 years. They had a good run, but those vows didn't make it a lifetime. I'm rarely in touch with any of that crew anymore. Our aisles have led in separate directions. I'm still embarrassed, though few attendees could recall my name. I'm just the out-of-town dickwad who ashed in the holy water. I suppose there may come a day when I'm questioned at the pearly gates and St. Peter will want to know if it's true, if I'm the one, if I'm the hooligan he's heard about, and what can I say? It was yours truly. I did it. But I quit smoking a long time ago. And serious drinking. And going to church too, for that matter, so it never happened again. That ought to count for something.

Regret Au Gratin, Longing Pie

Here at the lunch counter of what might have been, the menu is limitless, but you will always go hungry. There is the Paris you skipped in favor of Nice, and the funeral you missed to dally in Rome. The Apple investment you almost made. The turn at that motel instead of turning home. The *unsaid thank yous*, the *if onlys*, the *so much more you could have dones*.

But today's special is not the pilot's license you did not get nor the skydiving you meant to do, it is the woman in the yellow dress, sheer as the chiffon light that slants across those booths by the window, the woman who danced with you all night, then disappeared, borne back to her own borders of impulse and consequence, swept off by the flow, around the bend and out of sight, leaving only the faint smell of her hair and a vague remembrance of her face. And it does not matter if some 40 years have passed, if you were separated by distraction or she was somehow called away, she exists now as an entrée under *what could have been*, a lovely specter in the lineup of *we'll never knows*.

Does she ever think of you, remember you at all, from among the dozens she danced with in her lifetime, does she ever recall, as you do, your palms against her supple waist? Such simple mistakes. You back out of a parking space and journey left instead of right, and that, as the old man said, makes all the difference. And the here where you find yourself, so utterly dependent upon every decision you have ever made, that here, even now is a springboard to there, wherever you will wake tomorrow, thumbing the sleep from your eyes, hungry, thirsty, alone on your stool or not.

The decades pass one glance at a time, you breathe in and out, you set one foot before the other, one word in front of the other, you go on further into *things happen.* And you know you must let go, stop walking backward into the present, you must swivel on your stool and choose again who you are to be, but the memory will always waft there, a faint blur of gold in your peripheral vision, indeterminate, ghost-like, an apparition that trails along with you, not really behind you, but at your side, where she probably should have been.

Gasoline

Even all these years after the divorce, I still sometimes dream we are together. She and I will be rushing, hand in hand, late for a movie, or we will be planning our daughter's birthday, surrounded by cupcakes. In the dream, I actually know what is ahead, all the accusations and craziness, but there is something hopeful about the way she touches me, even still. I think there will always be a bond, even after so much betrayal. Even after the sting of those deceptions has passed. The children will always be our children. You would never undo that.

Ask me what these dreams mean to my life now and I don't have an answer. I have loved other women. I have failed other women and will undoubtedly continue to do so. One dream, I remember, had a security camera in one corner of the room. Its red light let me know that it was on. I leaned over then and kissed her. I wanted someone to see it, I think; I wanted the guard to know how it used to be for us. Or me, I guess, for me. But really, I don't romanticize the past all that much. I know how bad things got. I know she could never change. I know I tried, but didn't, and those are the stark facts. Our children wept. They were just babies, so shocked and confused. A moment like that leaves its scars on a person. It changes you chemically. Sometimes I suspect I am no good for anyone else. Not as if I were a dead end—more like I'm not even a road. I mean, she was not some incurable disease, but there is an inner skin I apparently can't shed. These simple things I dream; my spirit's way of reminding me what it was to feel that deeply, to love that much. You want that again with someone. With anyone. But you can never have it. You can only be destroyed like that once in your life. Nothing after will ever come close. After, you handle intimacy as if it were a dangerous fluid. You use approved containers. You don't smoke in the same room.

And maybe that is how to envision these dreams—as vessels for feeling. They help me carry her from one side of my life to the other. There is my little daughter with icing on her nose. There is the empty car seat that is still in the attic. There is my son learning to ride his bike on another man's street.

I am not a idiot. :) I know better than to pine for all that has vanished behind me. In fact, I am faced forward, usually; a striking picture of good health, braced headlong against the wind! Well, more or less. Still, I am surprised to be here. I thought my life would turn out differently. I expected better from and for myself. And so, though reconciliation isn't something I want to happen in real life, in my dreams, it's ok. In my dreams, nothing cruel or unforgiveable has transpired between us yet. In those dreams, it's that fresh and untouched. It is a pleasure to feel that fully again, to have the family under one roof. Even now, I like to think of that old guard monitoring the security cameras, him just noticing how nice it must have been. That's all I really wanted, was for life to be easy, right, fluid. It didn't seem like a lot to ask for at the time.

The Healing Potion

My nephew, lost in Luigi's mansion, boasts he will survive past level one, *even if it kills him.* All he must do is *progress*, he says, though what he means is *endure.* At eight, there is still a dim sconce of hope in his creepy hallway. But we know he'll blow his birthday money on another game, long before he's mastered this. What's new. There is always a leggy blonde cocktail in our headlights at the edge of the driveway, yes? Or a mysterious, cleft-chinned armful of roses? And when we sweep our meager penlights along walls, seeking hearts we stashed but can't now find, we soon discover where the bad ghosts hide. Exactly how many lives do we have left? Where can we search out the healing potion? Ask the wizard all you want—without his magic coin, you're screwed. Darling, I give. These freed stars are just sequins sparking against your vast black sky, one more midnight lit by a lover's fridge, its wedge of light untouched on the plate. But then, who is keeping score? And sweetheart, no one calls them joysticks anymore.

Grocery List

It is the old story. The precious toddler rides a pony for his birthday. When his mother gets distracted with other mothers, he falls off and breaks an arm. He fears horses and women for the rest of his life. The horse issue does not come up much. A little twinge watching westerns, maybe. No free rodeo tickets. Trusting women, however, is another matter entirely. It seems a prerequisite for happiness, no getting around it. One relationship after another, right in the toilet.

Finally, he goes to a therapist about this. A female one, no less. (That's giving it the good old college try.) She asks him to relax and close his eyes. He can barely even do that. He knows it is silly. What is she going to do? Pull him off the chair by his ankles? But he'd just rather know what she was doing every minute. Is that so wrong?

He closes his eyes and answers her questions. He can hear her rustling on her side of the coffee table. Is she frustrated? Is it his fault he can't remember every goddamn thing that ever happened to him? He barely remembers his social security number. But he's gotten this far, hasn't he? And what is she doing now? Crossing her legs again? Ok, she has made her point; he gets it already. And just what exactly is she writing in that notepad? All that scribbling cannot be good. But at least she seems intent on it—at least she is paying attention. All these questions are leading somewhere. She has her hands on the reins, so to speak. Have a little faith.

Epithalamion

(Niagara Falls)

Here his curtain of vows
    There her bride's veil of shadows
Here his Noh mask of steam
    There her bodice of rainbows
Here their decoupling confessional
    Of train and lace trestle
        Of foam-shrouded turbines
            Juicing rinds between worlds
Of fern fronds torn panties bird nests baits
    Splintered oars bobbers Styrofoam plates
Here the hallowed idyllic
    Drowns gnats by the million
        Each singular hymn
            Coerced and co-opted
Only gorged water
Only depths fraught with cold
Only the deafening choir of forced sublimation
    The baton-tapped orchestral dissolution of being
Only the literature of carcasses
    Story upon story into story
        Terror ecstasy tapestry
            Symphonic sheen and crescendo
Suspension extenuation conflation
The plaitings of fortune
Molten death mask of anonymity
The emptying of fulfillment
    The absorption of ending
        Rejoining unloosing lessening
As we is now and err will be
Alone in our unison
Halleluiah etcetera

Hindsight

Now that the tempest has tapered to a fine mist, now that regret's razor edge has been dulled smooth, I can admit at last how much I loved her and just how foolish I was to piss that love away, always thinking something better elsewhere, of someone else I'd yet to find. While she stayed faithful to a fault, to my faults, to be precise, I was fumbling with the keys to myself, drunk, often, inconsiderate always, a poor husband and lover, selfish and self-involved. Another woman benefitted from her misfortunes; I did my growing up with someone else. In fact, there were lots of women upon whom I inflicted myself, women whose only mistake was to trust me, however briefly, with their hearts when I could not even trust myself, before I learned the difference between what's real and what's imagined, before I knew my own foibles well enough to stop. It has taken much of my life to quiet my want, to appreciate a gift as it is given. There is a part of me that would like to tell her this, that would selfishly seek redemption, but who knows if she's alive. Would I even have the right to ask? Do I really want to know? Somehow it still matters. Somehow her death would still be a loss to bear. I'd rather go on picturing her in my own way—approaching old age with husband and grandkids, vital, content and sure she spent her life exactly as she should. Still true to the kind of loyalties I betrayed; far, far beyond any memory of me.

II.

SHELTER

Letter to Hoagland and Rivard from Wichita, KS, 5/3/98

Brothers, I can hear you cruising out there, passing a quart of Colt between Cambridge and Las Cruces. I would come along, but here beneath the tonnage of pull-ups and baby wipes, I keep nodding off. These days, I feel just vague, gnaw-finned nosings of my former life. Occasional Saturdays, I think a poem might be whistling from some sleek, chrome-splashed convertible, but it's usually just my minivan's fan belt going bad.

At sixteen, I would wheel through Our Lady of the Snows, sipping warm Pabst by the grottoes, smoking Pall Malls from the shrine lobby vending machine. Warm, humid wind. Summer's silk-lined arousals. For years, I had the windows all the way down, the world against my face, and that fast car was mine—bleeding oil, wounded paint—but mine. How wide and endless the pavement always was. Darkness rumbling up from balding, badly balanced tires, soaking through the floorboards, my questions a kind of fuel that propelled me night past night toward answers infinite as stars and therefore no answer at all.

Gentlemen, I hear your tireless singing out there above the finely tuned four-barrel of our generation; I envy how you've stripped the insulated wires to an ignition we weren't given keys for. I know the crack in your windshield runs clear through the whole complacent country.

Yet I'm strangely at peace now, writing rarely, lighting the small votive candles of my children, watching them flicker against their dim rooms, then flare into laughter and speech. And I rail against the shit-for-brains sixteen-year-olds who race on my street, against the hotheads who never stop for the bus. Playing chicken with the future, I was always going to be first to adjust.

It's getting late here in sleepy Wichita, my friends. All three kids are down. Karin is reading in bed (our queen-sized flotation device), so I am signing off—father, husband, professor, but barely poet, if I am precise. Whatever I manage for the record now—emails, bedtime tales, memos begging each 2% raise—may not be art but will have to suffice.

Shelter

You are seventeen and idling in the blown snow. All along the dark street, loose drifts cross from curb to curb, swirling and shifting like dust swept over stone. You can almost feel it as it passes beneath the car. It can't help but take part of you with it, far into the black depths beyond the streetlight. Beside you, the brick houses bear auras of red and green from Christmas lights, their color sparking as the windshield dulls then clears beneath the wiper blades. What is it about being cocooned within the steel, harbored from the cold that heightens everything? Breath clouding the window seems mystical. To exist as something more than a speck of snow seems a miracle.

Outside, the full brute force of winter is being borne. Animals are burrowed in their dens. People are bunkered in their homes. It seems only you are left to travel the unplowed roads, no lanes to guide you. What effort it took to clear the forests of this country. Roads paved today are the same routes once traveled by horses and wagons. You picture a landscape spotted with way stations and rough shacks, try to imagine living then. So much change has happened that even you have witnessed, driving still new to you—living itself, still new to you.

You have never been kissed the way your date kissed you tonight, open-mouthed, with ardor. Your own desire surprised you and has left you unguarded. You have felt her mouth on yours long since she left the car but won't see her now until school on Monday. She sits two rows ahead in History. You like looking at her hair and imagining her face when she answers questions in class. You will think now of her smile in a secret way. You might even grasp history more easily, having started to sense a place within it.

You can hear the ancient wind at work above the hum of the engine and the thud of wiper blades. You look again at the fuel gauge, which reads two-thirds full. You have shelter. Even stuck in a ditch, you could run the motor all night and never freeze. It is time for you to try for home. But first you must remember this scene, bury it deep in muscle and bone, safe beneath the skin. There will come a time you need it. There will come a season of grave damage, when your hair has grayed, and your will is weak and you are idling, alone, wherever abject need has led. And though it will be August, the air conditioning on high, a high sun sweltering, you will recall this moment and feel its blessing grace your lips.

Poem at Forty I Could Not Finish Until I Turned Sixty

The seas below our house pitch deep and soundless. Like sweat engrained in handrails, or the oil darkened edges of our dining room table, every shadow implies more shadow.

Late summer has quieted the cicadas, damped their dwindling number with the lastness of their deaths. There is a chill to the air, no wind at all. My youngest son is twenty days old, feeble, burrowing in and out of awareness, still unsure his body isn't trying to kill him. He cries to eat, he cries to sleep, he cries as his tiny gut rejects what all must go to waste.

Last week, scientists discovered the bones of a humanoid who fell into a well shaft three million years ago. His wife said he'd turn up! That the world has no pity for the individual life, this is no secret to anyone, yet we just can't get over it. I am here in the middle of a bed, in the middle of the night, in the middle of my life, my son nestled as if he were my own bones, as if we've both toppled forty years down into positions we'll retain forever. There is no chiropractor for the soul.

The museum of loss has at last opened its doors to me. Scholars cannot agree, the docents say, but almost certainly arms encircling the body was an omen of intimacy. Little is known of the fabled kiss; what remains of crude glyphs and mosaic shards indicate our elders once believed that souls were exchanged. One cannot, of course, touch anything in the museum of loss. One can only view what was once there. Nothing can be imagined and remain the same.

Just what does this portend? There will always be a thermos next to the detonator, a pair of reading glasses weighting the sentence handed down without mercy. An airman in WWII, John Ciardi recounted how once from the blister all gunners sat in, he watched the bomber beside him burning. His counterpart waved up as that other plane went down.

Each age has its designated bandwidth. Without warning, my son is twenty and in love. We are belted in. Splitting space. In his lap, he holds one hand with another, as if to keep its fingers from detaching, as if I'd helped him hurry to the car, and was driving to a hospital. *I want my tree back the way it was*, he whined, one autumn morning. He was four or so and knew even then what he's now not able to share.

Much is felt that resists being known. If there are seven billion human beings on earth, then every day is 19 million years of experience, just all at once. Somehow, I find this comforting, though by now you'd think we'd know what we are doing.

Short Cake

It is vanilla scooped on short cake again, centered in shallow sherbet bowls shaped like flying saucers. The room's tone is a mellow colonial butternut, burnished in sunlight from the wide kitchen window. Dusty plastic ivy trails from sconces on walls, while the family scoots in chairs around the table.

My grandmother is doling out food, as she would her whole life. And I, just a boy, have taken it with no thought of her future absence in my life, these years when I would feed myself, alone, in front of the TV, in a stark room without napkins and niceties.

It is late August 1966; the House Un-American Activities Committee is investigating Vietnam protesters for communist influence. The Red Guard has tortured Lao She for collecting art and has sanctioned mass murder throughout the whole of China. Three teens have been kidnapped and killed in Everman, Texas. While I am ten, wolfing sweets in Kansas where the sun has blanched my short hair even blonder, the crew cut so flat my toy helicopter could land on it.

Here, where tractors drive the streets more often than cars and weathered men and women are wresting a nation's supper from the hard-packed, merciless earth, we are giving thanks for our many blessings and packing on a few more ounces.

When it comes to freedom, things are well-water clear. We don't give a tinker's doodle about those commie retards. We think Medicare is a slippery slope. We think protestors have too much time on their girly hands. We think Negroes should quit whining and just get to work. We have enough on our plates, just worrying about ourselves. Besides this country, nobody's ever handed us anything.

Poses

(Colorado, 1964)

In this slide, a Native American family, or people hired to seem one, sit near a makeshift teepee and Conoco sign, posed for photographs and tips, helping to sell the souvenir tomahawks and moccasins. Their garb is finely crafted, its precise beadwork owing in heritage, probably, to multiple tribes and belonging, finally, to management, who takes it back at the end of each day. Especially impressive is the chief's feathered headdress, long and flowing off his shoulders as he holds my toddler brother in his buckskin arms. A young warrior looks on, the only nod to modernity a pair of Ray-Ban knockoffs he has daubed with war paint to match his face.

That's ok. We are all on board. There is, after all, a 24-hr. laundromat at hand, a grocery store and signs pointing out a payphone just over his shoulder. He would be about 72 years old now, which means statistically, it is likely he is dead. The life expectancy for Native American males is the lowest in America. But in this photo, he is vital and strong, with a proud bearing the elder chief has lost. Perhaps it is because the headdress doesn't fit and tilts a little sadly over the latter's eyes.

In the distance, rugged mountains slope off into the neatly forgotten, misbegotten past. That wilderness looms nobly beyond us, protected by national legislation. Meanwhile, down on the rez, Ute children skip double-dutch beside their shacks. How has it come to this is an insulting question. We know the answer. Really, it is quite clear to everyone. But that answer requires we admit who we are.

Happy Hour at the House of Tang

Once, during happy hour at The House of Tang, I watched as a foot-long parrotfish sprang from one aquarium, through the air and into another, clearing, in doing so, the coiffed hair of a short waitress and setting, I am sure, some kind of Chinese restaurant aquatic record. You just have to want it bad enough, we're told. Isn't that the American Dream? Anybody can do it, if you have the spunk! It has nothing to do with who you know on the zoning board or who will invest in state-of-the-art woks—it's all about chutzpah, about brass balls and elbow grease and bootstraps! While we patrons swarmed in our free-market school around complimentary appetizers and two-for-one wells, the real keepers were in the coral, trying to blend in, as best they could. The pious angelfish, decked out, yet aloof; the clownfish, all kissy face with her anemone sugar daddy; the cleaner shrimp, mopping up after everybody else; and every so often the pirate's treasure chest popping open, bubbles wriggling free from its plastic doubloons—I'm telling you it was paradise! Though, I may have exaggerated a tad about the parrotfish. It actually glanced off the lip of the second tank, flopping smack on a beleaguered bus boy, who plopped it, promptly, right back where it belonged.

Easter

Santa Rosa, '51 ~ pastel sky ~ static sun ~ hand sewn dresses ~ a promise kept ~ ribboned tresses ~ high church steps ~ post-world war ~ vintage year ~ the sisters squint ~ eyes tear ~ pallid yellows ~ stark white cross ~ blunted shadows ~ secret costs ~ behind that lens ~ a partial face ~ rough hands ~ no one knows about

Leftovers

In the photo, you can barely see her through the weathered screen door, watching her daughter walk away toward the camera, we kids packed into the backseat, ready to depart. My mother was leaving her childhood home yet again, and her mother was watching yet again, the youngest of her children, her baby, last to load into the car.

There is a set of linens in my mother's arms, a gift perhaps, something handsewn no longer needed at the farmhouse, or perhaps she has taken down clothing from the wash line; it is hard to tell, she holds them so closely to her chest and the photo is quite grainy. Whatever the case, my grandmother is lingering, ghost-like, watching us drive away. She is feeling a frayed rope of dust rise up from the long gravel drive and hover briefly before it sifts back deep into her lungs and the life she has left only once since 1910, when she visited her sister in Boulder and rode a train through the Rocky Mountains.

She was a mere girl then, not nearly even her daughter's age. Now she suffers a husband who rarely speaks and a routine of chores she completes in her sleep, a life as constant as the Kansas wind that sweeps across the soybean fields, drying out everything and everyone—that leaves a thick film of topsoil on every human good, as if to reclaim it for our lord God's greater purpose.

In truth, she can't tell what she clings to, from what she's stuck with. There is the family bible humped open near her rocker. There is the waist-length hair her arthritic hands can barely braid. There is the kitchen she can scarcely turn around in, the squat refrigerator slumped in a living room corner. She's never had running water; she pumps what she needs from their well in the yard. Here at the door, she mostly appears some wan spirit evanescing in the back-ground, one hand held to her throat, the other to her heart, as if she were quietly gasping for air.

Meet my grandmother, née Ida Knudson. She unbunches her old house dress. She shifts and smooths her apron, re-ties its strings and returns to the turkey in the kitchen. Nothing more must go to waste. It is November 1964. Thanksgiving has come and is over for everybody else, but she will pick at this carcass until her whole bleak life is bone.

Birthday Money

The child is holding up her birthday money. It is fourteen dollars, for seven years. This is what she always gets from her grandpa, her age in two-dollar bills, crisp new notes, he went to the bank to get just for her. He leashed his dog and walked the four blocks downtown to the quaint branch office where he does his business. They know him there, though one teller mistakenly calls him Walt and he never corrects her. This has been his gifting habit for years. He doesn't have a lot of money, but he owns his house, and the taxes are low, so he makes out just fine. His granddaughter will never know about the stone bench by the courthouse. He likes to sit there for a bit, after using the mailbox and before walking home. The squirrels are always industrious in the surrounding trees. The young people are always passing in and out of the county offices, getting marriage licenses and building permits, paying fines or serving on juries.

His granddaughter's cake this year is shaped like a butterfly and has coconut sprinkled in the yellow icing. She is almost two thousand miles away, but he has received this picture via email. She looks genuinely happy, he thinks. The bills are spread out in her hand like a fan or like she is playing a game of Go Fish. No telling what she will buy with it. Kids now have so many choices. As long as she is happy, he thinks, that's what's important. Walter has come to appreciate email. Sure, he feels nostalgic for the post offices he grew up with, but he only uses mail for the cards, really. He thinks there is a lot his parents missed, relying on sporadically mailed snapshots. Walter rarely saw his own grandparents. He knows now how poor they were. But he always looked forward to the stick of Juicy Fruit in his cards. He still feels lucky. Walter's daughter sends jpeg files often. He feels like he sees the children changing day by day. He's watched his daughter, too, growing older, getting a tinge of silver in her hair. She looks more like his late wife every year, a fact that used to cause a twinge in him but doesn't anymore. She's a trooper, that one—four kids and a husband who changes jobs like socks. Still, look at that cake! Look at those smiles! Those seven bills a signal that all is well, that he is of value, that he is remembered, no matter what.

All Right

The boy doesn't know what to do. He's only twelve. And he's never seen adults weep, not like this at least, so distraught, disconsolate. He can see his grandmother from the kitchen, through her bedroom doorway. Prisoner of her dementia, the old woman lies fully clothed atop the chenille bedspread, her floral house dress faded, her shoes scuffed and worn, light from one window cutting her in two. Her good dishes have disappeared, the piano is still in the old farmhouse, the cows need to be milked, her young sons are still in France at war. The boy sits at the breakfast table, adrift in a sunlit swirl of dust motes. He understands none of this is true, but how is he to help? What can anyone say? To live is to leave, the boy thinks; we make our way, but lose something always and wherever we go. Our shoe soles wear down, our hair thins, our bodies diminish and so we travel always through galaxies of our own shed lint and skin, the leavings of once known things. Finally, at a loss, he just lies down next to her, his sneakers alongside her purpled ankles. He knows nothing ever is going to be all right, but he says it anyway.

Author, Author

He has spent his life with books, but now that he is long retired, he doesn't want even the few shelved around his apartment. He won't pick one up, even if it occurs to him. He's stopped writing, too, after 50 years of daily practice, every morning, without fail at the desk. He has simply had his fill of words. It hasn't been difficult to quit a lot of habits. Smoking, for instance. Hospitalized twice, it simply became so poisonous he had to. And the booze, well, that doesn't really count. He is so thin he can't tolerate much. One can't really call it drinking.

One gets used to having nothing to do. He has his TV, his hole in the ice, and he sits close, as if at a window. People pass by, going about their lives. Young, fresh-looking families propelled from one activity to another. If he ever had the energy for that, he can't recall it now. He likens himself to the rubber bands swept out of his office desk drawer, some used so often they had lost elasticity, others so dried up they crumbled in two. That said, he still showers, shaves, dresses as if driving to campus each morning. His father taught him that much. Of course, he doesn't even *have* a desk in this puny apartment space. He couldn't really work, even if he wanted.

He had been an extraordinary writer, eight books altogether, well known and respected by the best authors of his day. Three novels. Four volumes of stories, even one of poems. But no one reads his work now. Who wouldn't feel bitter? So many highs and lows. He emptied himself out onto the page, year after year, story upon story. There had been intense passion and utter rejection. He had paid his tributes to language and the gods of art; he had approached greatness. But nothing rests merely on merit in this life. There is always the rule of preferential attachment. You have to catch a break in this business. A well-timed moment that can snowball enough to never melt.

He is sequestered now, ill, his children scattered across the country, his wife remarried in another state. The student or two who keep in touch are either more successful than he or struggling with their own anonymity. Their occasional emails keep him from feeling completely forgotten. So much of his life was spent in the classroom. He takes some solace in thinking that he did some good there, had some impact on other lives. Perhaps others found his fiction revelatory, too. Perhaps. But those years are long past. No one calls for advice anymore, nor does he understand the current scene well enough to offer it. Some days this matters more than others.

Nothing lasts. This is the main lesson. We are taught it with the first embrace, with the first experiences of hunger; so much of what we do is just an effort to duplicate some original feeling or experience that cannot be had again. Nothing lasts. He runs through the channels. One commercial after another embraces some new change in products or technology or thought. It's tiresome, actually. He doesn't have it in him. It is physically exhausting just to sit and watch.

For Phil Levine

My teacher had studied with Philip Levine, so it was in college I first read *1933*. That book both thrilled and angered me in a selfish way, because I loved the poems, but resented that he'd done what I longed myself to do. Child that I was, I refused to read him again for seven years, certain I needed to teach myself whatever he knew. . . . But it was too late, as it always is, whatever we take in, we absorb for good, we synthesize and transpose, we splice, we carry forward. And it would be Levine, years later, who laid the sword on my shoulders; it was his opinion that would matter. Don't misunderstand. We wrote, we talked, but we were not close. I was no acolyte. He was no mentor. I witnessed him generous and impatient and even unkind. But his judgments, renowned for candor, would always matter greatly. He was a natural force, as poems themselves are. One line links to another; a vital system, a body, emerges on the page.

Phil Levine died this week. His missteps died with him. His humanity is what will be remembered—the bone and blood of his poems, their poignant and vulnerable relations, their insistence on saving every name of the lost. Yet even so he is gone. One turns the page now knowing we must make do with what he left. I am growing old, myself. My brief world within the world stutters on, though at a loss for words, as often as not. In fact, they rarely flow as they did when I was young. I thought the well was depthless once, I thought there would be no end to them, but some mornings now, it seems there's little left to share. This is worrisome. It reflects a lack of energy for the greater good; it bespeaks a vision settling for its own limits.

But then, all I have to do is project myself into Phil, even for a moment. To see him in his youth, say, loading a boxcar, cartons of pop bottles trembling against one another, stacks accruing, the individual bottles glinting beneath the vapor lamps of the railway yard; Levine here within them, just another container among the many, one rattling voice in the multitude, struggling to make himself known . . . All it takes is one good nudge to put me here, where he goes on loading and stacking and dreaming, while somewhere in this monument to consumption and sweat labor and shared lives, some bottles have broken, spilling orange Faygo, and soda leaks now from the door's edge, draining from the boxcar, dribbling down into the gray chat pocked with boot prints, sweetening the bitter earth of Detroit.

The Guardian

He can carry the pistol here if he pleases. It's legal. It is his own home, after all. So, if he wants to sit down to the kitchen table with it right on his belt, well, more power to him. It's not that he lives in a particularly dangerous neighborhood. It's not that he's old or frail or vulnerable due to illness and the like. No, he's just tired of being small. Sometimes, alone at night, he watches cop shows and imagines being the victim of a crime. How surprised his attacker would be! The brute would break in expecting to find a thickset, asthmatic accountant only to be held at gunpoint, humiliated, until the authorities could arrive! In these daydreams, Vincent never imagines actually firing the gun. In truth, he has never even taken it to a range; in truth, it took him days to muster the nerve to load the magazine and rack a round into the chamber.

As a boy, he'd been left out. Even his brothers ditched him, abandoning him to video games and TV's make-believe. He grew comfortable with role-play—always it was easier being someone else. Adult fantasies are no different. After the foiled robbery, he is lauded as an upright, stalwart citizen. He is even on the local news at six. Sometimes single neighbor women stop by with food in tinfoil and Tupperware containers. They've put on fresh makeup. The smell of their perfume lingers in his entry for hours. He wears his gun when he comes to the door, too. The women, he thinks, pretend not to like this, but really, they appreciate feeling protected. That is what he is: he is a guardian.

It is when he starts to believe this that he first slips the pistol into his briefcase before work. He should have it with him, just in case. You just never know. Stranger things have happened. And what if someone were to be fired and go postal, as they call it. Sometimes during the workday, he fingers the grip to remind himself it is there, tucked beneath file folders and the detritus of office life. He imagines his co-workers cowering under their desks while he rushes to their aid. Quiet, unassuming Vincent. Who would have thought! Of all people.

Who knows when it begins to go bad. When he first realizes that nothing dramatic is going to happen. His life is not going to change. *He* has changed, he has become a heroic figure, willing to risk his life for theirs, but no one will ever notice. He can see clearly now how they ignore him, take him for granted. Good old Vincent, always arriving 15 minutes early, often as not, the last to leave. Give it to Vincent. He'll do it. He'll have it on time without a word of complaint. Yes, good old, thorough, steady, Caspar Milquetoast Vincent. . . . Eventually, there are outbursts in client meetings; there is shattered crockery in the breakroom. Eventually he tells his cocky supervisor what he truly thinks of him.

He is made to take a *voluntary* leave. His apartment becomes more cramped and cloistered. He receives no visits beyond take-out delivery and his world grows more austere. He often finds himself facing the TV, his finger on the trigger, taking aim at one big shot or another. Neighbors later said they heard him exclaim at all hours of night and day, and never glimpsed him retrieving his mail. At some point, he let his fish starve and stopped paying bills.

Afterward, Channel 2 posted a personnel head shot from when he first joined the firm. He looked young and fresh. He had a boyish smile. The woman who had snapped the photo, a survivor, remembered thinking he was sweet, in a reserved sort of way. Quiet, unassuming Vincent. Who would have thought? Of all people.

III.

WHAT IS THIS THEN BETWEEN US

Storm Front

August, late summer's whelming green foliage in the backyard, yet children's voices carry far, for decades it seems, from private pools and the park. Simple, timeless games. Hide and seek. Keep away. Shrill yelps of disappointment or pleasure, mostly you can't tell which. Certainly, not who. And so, my one long-lighted evening in the garden has led unerringly to this: ageing in a young neighborhood, stirred by voices I dreamily mistake for my own children. They could be crossing the creek. They could be coming home from school through the patch of high grass between houses. An early milestone, that day, finally deemed old enough to walk themselves.

Muffled, but powerful and plainspoken, like a heavy duffel dropped after a long journey, comes thunder. Soon after, the wet hiss of water. Then, as suddenly as the rain starts, the voices desist, vanished inside to their separate provinces. I miss my sons and daughter, but then I have always missed them, even when I held them. I was always reminding myself to be present, to demarcate significance. I was always a little lost within my own home. A form of Narcissism, I suppose, never feeling able to take in enough. Honestly, I fear now, as I become old, both remembering too little and too much. Either pitfall bears challenges.

Yesterday, watching a video of my youngest at two or three, listening to my young, robust voice read his storybook, I found I couldn't breathe. I would never be that father again; those years were lost to me. I understood then how such panic takes one to the edge of living. There is a violence enmeshed in memory I do not fully comprehend; ends are implicit in it.

And yet there is such gentleness just now in this light rain, coming as it has after a long, flushed afternoon of play, even the birds stilled. Has the rain brought erasure, or has it enjoined a bottomless remembrance? Both? Dear lord, there is such acute risk in loving anything at all, in allowing something to matter. One strike of lightning could disrupt the power, could wipe this screen clean. Yet, I refuse to click save until the end. Why pretend to save what cannot be salvaged? Why not just let go?

Just outside my open window, the waters of someone's heaven filter down through the leaves. Those voices, my children, my past—I am saturated utterly by this subtle shower, become sodden with grief. But just when I think I cannot bear it, the birds start to call for each other again. They know before I do that the worst has passed by and barely grazed us. Soon the world will set about drying again. Children will venture out, resuming their play.

Song for the Outer Doors

Beautifully caged, well preened set prop, the stout finch turns from its imported seed. Then, unfazed by the sound stage of mirrored swings, indifferent to the sprung wire hatch of the starlet's limousine, it sings.

Born, bred and all too soon, dead indoors, as were its forebears and theirs before. A celluloid symbol of snug domesticity, an unexalted extra, yet with a theatrical lineage traceable, kernel by kernel, to a seminal, much lauded silent film with subtitles for a family song. The only voice here inherited for the sky is a gleam deep in the property room, in the gilded harp's one golden wing.

Therefore, cued and poised above an ever-evolving parlor, it sings again— dutifully, happily—exactly what it knows. Even if there are—when well-heeled moguls come and go—those brief, unsettling drafts, that oddly stirring light.

In Medias Res

The sky is chalked a powder gray. Vascular limbs seep black across and the roof shingles lie smothered beneath that heaven's weight. A girl's cat steps eternally from the porch's slab, her tail low, her right paw outstretched, the grass forever brittle with December's cold. Everything is at the edge of change. The front door will always be just about to close. The pallid world in the storm door's pane will always be just on the verge of shimmering, pattern wrested from endless flow. The girl's face will always be an entryway, walls of burnished butternut within her. The empty birdcage. The dusty plastic ivy dribbling from sconces. Another family forged around its ordained table. Generation to generation, the stark condiments passed. This is fifty years ago. The girl's father is 46. Her mother is 43. One strand of Christmas bulbs bows in segments below the eaves. Leaves from the hardwoods need to be shaken from the evergreens. Even now, nut hulls need be raked into piles. Cup your hands around your eyes. Gaze down into the deepening glass. Everything is about to change. Everything depends upon some other fluid thing. Someone leaving and someone staying. A neighbor wrings her undergarments. A neighbor harms himself. Help may or may not arrive. The ambulance may or may not need its siren. What the girl believes will prove to be unimportant. The soul insists on being let out. The neighbors' dog whimpers to be let in. The cat sniffs at the air.

Epic

After ever, the fall winded of apples and high now for grass. The bruised inness of else and complete all. Once but was way long there a trial, journey far atoward the overmore and more ever of each the said all. Versa vice of or for two loves never naught between twice—hail thrall stranger house, long hall quest of heroic once havings happened. Atwist altogether this way then those than others. Danger in patience they require, such as it such, the allless every—the thing more of less, our ration air thin or adwindle. God us, then grant that heart leastways at wisdom, an enview to tale that is the unseen of of it all that is. That there then there, the forafter being this and always, though not for all in ever.

Creation Myth

I will keep on walking, don't think I won't. Don't tell father, he'll get the strop. Don't tell mother, she will get the brush. Say it's for the razor. Say it's for her hair. Tell them I didn't do it. Say you best beware. I will keep going, don't think I won't. I will stay on my feet, swollen in the current. I will stay on my legs, which only look like they are broken. Cross, child, cross. Keep on your way. Father, I hear your thunder, but I am not listening. Mother, I feel your wind, but I am not listening. Because history is a journey family has no say in. Because memory is a lie, it is all refraction. Because heaven is a lie, no smoke returns to its fire. I will keep on my way, don't think I won't. I will be born. I will bear myself from my own bitter womb. Father, stand back. Mother, stand aside. This crossing was bound to happen. Because that is what it is to make and be made. Or why else will I have lived and died on this earth.

Sunning

There is no one left to tell who this comely girl was, no use irritably reaching after fact. Suffice it to say she knew us to some degree, perhaps better than in passing, as she seems to be somewhat aware of us there, so near the water's edge, still wet from swimming—she seems concerned as to our whereabouts. We are children, after all, my brother and I, on another vacation *away from it all*, as our parents liked to say, far from the bustling metropolis of Belleville and encamped in the environs of a true berg—a one gas station/bait shop/general store town—on the outskirts of which were a state park and boat ramp, family friendly campgrounds for the broad middle class who hooked up squat trailers to 110 A/C, then adjusted their antennae to watch the Cardinals on TV.

The girl has set off into the river alone. Of all here, she is the daring one who trusts her own footing on the slick stones beneath the shallow current—of all her siblings, say, she might be the last to marry. She angles both arms out for balance, as if walking a wire across some formidable canyon, but clearly aims toward a rock mound in the river's minor rapids. Head turned, a smile glows on her face, and I mean this literally, her teeth look radioactive in the sun.

What fate befell her we can only surmise, but she took it head up, this girl, whatever it was, she took it eye to eye. It is clear she has the backbone to bear time's crude betrayals, though her shoulders seem ever so slightly bowed, for it is hard enough to be faced with this brindled expanse of river and her newly swelling breasts and awkward feeling hips—hard enough just wading from place to place in this life, stiff current against you and your next step uncertain.

When she reaches those rocks, she will sun there, the river sweeping past on either side; worry will pause, while the world roils on without her. Let the river evaporate and fill. Let the body's cells slough and be replaced. Let the future wait for you and me to see. She can cease *becoming* for an afternoon and simply be.

What Is This Then Between Us

It is Reggae Night at the Brown Derby Grill and young people wash over me, wave upon wave. Feral amongst others, moving without thought or doubt, we brush and pull away, whirl off and return, we merge amongst the thrashing of strangers. I don't know it, but this will be the last time ever I feel so whole in my skin, completely at ease with how I seem to others. There is much I've yet to learn, much I will never learn, and some lessons I will only come to later, but I am present here, completely, and in sync with my kind. I have, for one night, no singular life. I am meshed with a vortex of ancient rhythms, the gift of simply being within one's given time on earth. I can hear music as I write this almost forty years hence; it's a marvel this band even toured in Vermont, especially then, in the dead cold of December. Outside, the snow piles deep, encrusted with mud, and the ice along the roadway is thick and pocked with gravel. But inside, we castaways enjoy an island summer—a salt breeze coarse in our hair, aquamarine water spread placid to the horizon. Foreign and exotic, unabashedly sexual, we seem driven by eruptions of some vital force. The band, too, can sense they've loosed something essential. They play without break or pause, blurring songs one into another, passing twined energies back and forth, maintaining the pitch as if it were a height they might never attain again, though it cannot be sustained, though it can and must end. Then suddenly it does. The band says good night. The overheads go on. And there are our coats, hanging heavy on a long row of pegs. There are the deer head trophies on the wall, the knots in pinewood paneling, the cedar bathroom doors. Here are the pallid faces of those we have danced with, their smiles ebbing, eyes accustoming to florescent light. Are we changed? Are we bettered? Will we live altered, day by day? Who am I to know or say. We spend such energy in protecting the self, so much time is wasted, so often we are exhausted. But there are touchstones in our short lives, moments held dear and never forgotten, and I suspect this night will be one for many. Togetherness, reassurance, however fleeting, are precious. We're only granted one dance, but need not face that alone.

When Calls the Heart

He's 6' 5" and 300 pounds now, but for the moment, he rides my sister as if she were a horse. About two years old and two seconds from sliding off, my brother Roger looks terrified, actually, there in his absurd string tie. But this made great sense at the time, all three siblings clad in Western wear, me alongside, strapped with six guns and a Bowie knife. My sister, Susan, is the oldest, probably ten, steady enough on hands and knees for the time required to get this photo taken.

Timing, after all, is all. When everything is spilling over from one moment into the next, you have to pause it anywhere you can. Something George Kodak understood. Just how relentless the future is. Witness the slight glare off my grandmother's plastic slipcovers. She worried so much about making that sofa last, we kids could rarely sit on it. And where it is now, 57 years after the fact, who in hell knows. There *are* people who save furniture that long. I know, I was raised by two of them. My mother has been cutting my father's hair for decades. I am 62, and he still sits, towel tucked around his neck, on the stepstool I was propped on as a toddler. How's that for a sentence, Mrs. Schiele? The older one gets, the more difficult syntax becomes. It is a chore trying to keep the world in order. Again, you have to resist time whenever you can. I must have sensed this even then. I look either soulful or confused, I am hard pressed to choose. There might as well be a caption bubble just above my head: *Unresolved issues with loss*.

Which is true. Who would I be if you took nostalgia away from me? Given the choice between the past and the future, I'll pick the past every time. It doesn't matter if that past was difficult. My children are grown, but I'd feel better if they were all home sick from school—hell, I'd prefer that they were still wearing diapers. Who says you have to let go?

Some change is probably helpful, however. Susan, for instance, doesn't want to be a horse anymore. And though I remain both soulful *and* confused, I no longer wear a gun at the dinner table. Turns out my brother, the bareback rider, would change the most. He takes no shit from anyone. Try getting him on a horse now, I dare you. My grandmother, may she rest in peace, has just six feet of upholstery to worry over now. And my mother, who exists in this snapshot as two disembodied, outstretched hands poised twixt Roger's noggin and the hardwood floor, has stopped trying to save everyone. When you're in your nineties, who has the oomph for that? Who can bear discerning order from chaos? Better to just wrap snug and surf the Hallmark Channels. "When Calls the Heart," to be exact. "All the time," being the answer.

Mortal Currents

Side against side ~ lain face-up in sleep ~ two lone clouds ~
one a stuffed bear ~ one my young son ~ across the ridge they
are passing ~ shorn apart ~ thinned to wisps ~

Little sleeper, dear child ~ so far from me now ~ there are
but these few miles of peace ~ these brief wondrous nights ~
then we wake diminished ~ awash in mortal currents ~

My son, sweet boy ~ this is such precious time ~ sleep long ~
churn deeper ~ dream ~ while you still own your face ~ while
you are still near to home ~ before the angel of forgetting ~
puts its cool lips to your eyelids ~ and you become a man

Coming of Age

Let me explain what I can: Lonnie Parker, whose last name I remember only in the fluid act of writing the first, needed two lanes to drive us both to work, two lanes and sometimes the shoulder, and we were not traveling freeways. You would not think a man could physically twist his torso like that, but he did not trust mirrors, nor neighboring cars, and so when looking left and right and front and back—all along yammering about wrongs harshly done him—he gyrated behind the steering wheel of his beaten blue Ford Falcon, a seething cloud mass of self-consciousness, boozed up, coke-laced, ready for another long day of painting whatever we were told to.

I was an old soul in a young man's body, and by that I do not mean patient, wise, or spiritual, I mean empty, exhausted and on the verge of surrender, but Lonnie could gab enough for both of us, there was always something to be railed against, usually the endless conspiracies against him, and how no one understood, not even his bitch sister, always judging his trajectory, in her picture-perfect house with her sissy husband.

Lonnie knew a good time when he saw one, whether at bars or through binoculars trained on beach chairs at the girls' dorms. He was a misdirected flame suspended ten yards from the flame-thrower after the trigger had already been let go. That is, he was headed nowhere and barely resisting being sucked back into the barrel of the world that spat him out. When I gaze now into the glass globe of zig-zagging electrical charges that he was, I predict doom and sorrow for the schmuck who once, after rehab in Oklahoma, got a farrier's license, schooling himself, in of all things, horses.

But in 1983 he was in Connecticut, wildly unhappy, and we made quite a pair, there in the swerving car, our souls two luggage tags with no names on them, attached to bodies we abused in dank, shitty rooms brightened only by curtains women made for us, surviving on their love and pity, and, in Lonnie's case, some promise his sister had made to their parents.

I, of course, did not live with him, in fact, I lived with my version of his sister; a good, if misguided, woman who'd chosen to love a selfish man, and who was suffering her choice, trapped in a demeaning job and a home life that revolved around our thorough dysfunction. And as she would for at least six more years, she was planting her twenties in garden beds and flowerpots around the 800-square-foot house we shared—unmarried, childless, and unequipped to grow up.

Lonnie was not an unintelligent man, he just couldn't control his mouth any better than the rest of his body, and this failure with language we also shared. My relationship to words was different—I wrote—but I was just as wildly voluminous and self-involved on paper as he was in the flesh. And because I never told him to shut up and to shit-can his incessant whining, he liked me somehow, and did not rant at me, the way he did some foremen. And so we were, at that moment, a two-man crew, painting Caribbean blue the water towers of a campus abrim with lives we both disdained and envied.

If I had truly listened to Lonnie, I would recall more about him now, but I didn't, so I don't. His life was not a story so much as a charged atmosphere, a tumultuous, angst-ridden storm. Though, at times, he shared a sweet, vulnerable side, as if strongly suspecting there was a crap-load he did not understand. And he was present in ways I, busy proving I could survive myself, found it hard to be. I see now how I denied my unforeseen future. I was just paying my dues, waiting to get started.

Son, I'm not sure how much of the paint I have slapped on in this life remains intact, but the fence I built in 1981 had been torn down last time I passed through Connecticut. Some memories, they are like fences, the boards perfectly parallel, not touching, but seeming continuous from a distance of several years. Who was that young man, with my name, paralyzed in the webbed lawn chair and that enclosure? What did I imagine when it was cold and I sat smoking in the backyard, my breath visible, the stars blur-edged through it? All I remember is a deep heaviness, like the lead apron at the dentist's—sometimes comforting, sometimes suffocating—moist with the exhalations of the living and the dead.

Ultimately, what advice can I offer? Stay open. Square your shoulders. Brace for the blow. Hope to get a look at what it is that hits you. Don't grieve over absence when there was nothing there to begin with. You will have to gouge out a place in this world, knowing there is no cure for what you feel, out there, where perspective stops short, blending into that blankness we slowly fill to understand. It is your job to wake the world every morning, to step again onto the porch, beyond which the lilies may be raised up like satellite dishes, just listening, like you. But then don't let metaphor muddy clear water. Always they are lilies and, like you, they are already all they need to be.

My Grandmother's Urine

Fun Cox family fact: my kids came to be
in the same bed my mom was conceived in.
Not the mattress, that would be gross,
but the once gilded cast iron frame
engendering rust in my garage, which,
to my shame, I will neither part with
nor paint. We should all have such quaint
record of our origin's coordinates—
a sort of carnal memorial
to our immodest beginnings.
Within these amorous parameters,
such a plaque might read,
two sparks joined in sacred flame! Ok,
so perhaps it was more of a pilot light,
but who wants to equate oneself
with a water heater or gas grill?

No, we, good sir or madam,
must be far beyond ordinary,
one of those wrens perched on a teeter totter
who truly expects something to happen.
We are deer partaking from the cattle's
water trough, the reflected whirring windmill
haloing our doe-eyed faces. We are
Aunt Edith's wedding ring found
in a prairie shithouse, a Norway
license plate nailed to a Kansas barn,
quartz crystals nestling
in a warped cigar box.

But what, you might well be asking,
does all this have to do with
my grandmother's pee, which,
let me tell you, still stinks
some sixty years later, triggered

just by looking at this bed.
Disgusting, you say? Well, hey, you live
without running water for eighty years
and see how you manage! Imagine yourself
aged, frail, avoiding that outhouse
during storms, in the dark, in the snow,
on land you farmed, but never owned,
and squatting over a bucket at 3 a.m.

We plod our way with what we have
in this life. This was a wife whose
kitchen was smaller than a modern
clothes closet, and whose refrigerator
took up most of her living room. This was
a mother who fried her own hens' eggs
on a wood-fired stove and flipped them
with a fork, never breaking a yolk.

What, for you, constitutes the scent of loss?
When you hear the word *grandma* what
makes you reminisce? For me, it's not
crisp bacon or some pricey eau de toilette.
What I find most poignant is her piss—
the crude, seasoned essence of a stoic lifetime,
of an ordinary, unsung woman
who is greatly missed.

IV.

WONDER BREAD

Romantic Interlude #2

One neighbor, he thinks you're happy,
that you're clapping to a polka
he just can't hear,
and another neighbor,
that you're tipsy
and being maestro again,
gesturing to the orchestra pit
of evening peepers and crickets,
crescendoing and diminuendoing,
when really, it's the mosquitos,
desperate for the blood
of your neck and face,
and you are swatting them from the air,
crushing them between your palms,
hell bent on killing each
and every goddamn one of them.

Hubris

At first, just its sun-faded gills, perhaps,
or the one dull shirt snap of an eye,

but in the end,
even the most wary fly

will pause to comb its legs
in the mounted trout's mouth.

Oh yeah, uh huh, who's your daddy?!

How blithely we suppress our instincts,
then suffer, astonished,

the taut web trembling
between fortune's teeth.

Snare

The wire snare trembles,
trimmed with blood and fur.
Emptied earlier
by fox or bird of prey,
its loop glistens in suspense,
while inches away,
on red splotched snow,
the rabbit's torn and ravaged skin
is likewise enlivened
by fits of wind.

Newly warmed, empurpled,
the sky's full circle waits,
one low-slung cloud now baits
the lure of day. This
is the price we pay
for freedom beneath the sun:
to have lived an allotted time
and then be done;
to have been sheltered amongst many,
but to die as one.

I huddle over words,
I scratch and peck.
My life becomes this nest
of lettered keys.
Is there any home we're able to protect?
A shadow passes over
and I freeze.

Knowing

There beyond the picture window, framed by gold curtains, the forest could be on a museum wall. Stock-still, as they say. No flitting birds to be discerned. Not a single leaf twinged by wind or rain, not one busy squirrel bounding between limbs. Overnight, though, some trees have changed, the hues at their center newly dimmed. Or perhaps there has been a shift in him? That is not so easily ascertained, let alone explained. How long can smoke in a bottle remain smoke? Enlightenment visits briefly and in varying degrees. Always, by the time you grasp it, there is nothing to say.

Meantime, autumn continues unabated. Somewhere, fattened bears retreat to dank dens. A red fox glides along hedgerows as if on grease. The perched owl waits patiently for field mice to present themselves. What, friend, are we waiting for? What innate genetic code can we expect to manifest our lives? What grace shall we aspire to? Fire, perhaps, the wintry blaze of hearth or stove. Or story. Or mournful tune. Better, he thinks, to mind this silence and stasis, the eons old rock jutting steadfast up midst roots and leaf-fall. Better to resist the flux and believe that something stays. At last, he thinks, that is his answer. How still it all is, so utterly clear. Then one bright leaf lets go and changes everything.

Blink Once for Yes

Oncoming dusk. With each heave of wind, day's light lessening, a cooling of the ocean's sky-tinged water. Time slows and perception skews.

So it is, swaying palms tattoo the hotel pool's surface, and the duet from the thatched tiki bar dulls to a distant childhood, the submerged banter of adults over pinochle, neighbors calling to their wayward dogs.

Cars on the distant bridge now seem your mother's ant-riddled roses. A gull's shrill call seems the root cellar's rusted hinge. In that other universe of speckled linoleum, a galaxy sizzles and spits in a pan and her gray hair unbraids strand by strand.

Must there be no windfall after death's passing? Is there not one border of darkness we need not cross? The names of the lost are a second loss. All we embrace will die in our arms, and this is the burden, the unwieldy vacant clothes you must carry for folding.

Someone must serve as last witness, remove the wedding bands, unclasp the family brooches and fraternal pins. Someone has to map the cartography of stains, the orgy of throw pillows, the handsewn quilts with seams like old scars. The conga lines of overcoats, the xylophone of shoes, the untold husks of attempted selves.

Someone will have to face the ancient story chain-smoking on her steps, no key left under the mat, then lie back in the run on sentence of all that has taken place, in the still damp cursive of rumpled linens, grateful for the fact of feeling.

You are, after all, alive. There are, after all, worse fates than cool, blue water and a bourbon-rocks sweating near a plush towel and the tan legs of a woman who knows your middle name. No one can tell you what the end looks like. But you will know it when you see it.

Shroud

From Grace, in love, out of favor, asleep—
falling, it's said, because one feels
the profound slant of experience,

those gravities through which we've toppled
toward our separate selves—that otherness
in which we're wound at birth—

one's last face always latent in the first,
our deaths worn through life
like a second skin.
                                        Sometimes,

waking between sheets,
I am a boy on the beach again,
my face alone visible, soothed

by the press of damp coarse sand
and the force of my brother's hands,
as he scoops and packs the heaped mound.
                                                                        Sometimes,

waking to the silence of an empty house,
I hear what's beyond us, seep right
through to the ocean in everything.

Just so, chicks, barely hatched,
know instinctively not to move
when a hawk's shadow glides over them.
                                                                  Just so,

as if that shroud of sand,
those semi-human contours,
were a cloud levitating
in the azure and gold-tinged tropical sky,

the body quiets and stills, sensing now
how each breath is the volume of time itself,
that it will diminish, like the years,
exhalation by exhalation.

There is just one thing we can say we know.

Inform the dirt of your impatience.
Advise the seas in re the self.
Instruct the waterfall as to emptiness.

Talk to the river about your life's free course.

Silver Springs

It is the early sixties. High summer. The Florida sun is warm on their lower backs, not shaded by the canopy. They are at Silver Springs, peering down past tennis shoes through a glass-bottomed boat where water looks cool and clear as air against that glass, and fish school in and out of view with a panoramic flair. It is their yearly vacation time. They have been travelling as a family for almost two weeks—kids squabbling in the backseat, counting license plates and livestock; parents in front talking road maps and Texaco stations. But today is something special, today they are silent and drift the shore like petals along a gutter.

Each year, they have a few days to experience new things. They get away from their usual lives and see how others live—which is elsewhere, of course, and less well, mostly. It is an expensive lesson; they know this from the budget sheet completed each evening in the motel. It shows how successful they are being, staying within their limits. It tells them when they have treats at Stuckey's and when they don't. They should be grateful, the parents remind them. They are very fortunate. They have worked hard and lived frugally to earn what God has provided. Their car is late model and large, their clothes are the newest styles, their motel rooms are clean and air-conditioned. Their friends at home all seem to be prosperous, too. But then they drive by the shanties and the trailer parks and weather-thrashed houses with boards for windows. What is it with God, the boy has to wonder, how does he choose? If they had a budget, his dad says, they wouldn't have to live like this. But who teaches you that? And why does it seem to be a secret? People want things right away, his dad says, and make poor decisions. They should be saving for important things and investing in their future; instead, they spend on immediate whims that make them happy. Take beer and cigarettes, for instance. People don't need those to live. But somehow, the boy understands they do—just as he needs to look at his baseball cards before he goes to sleep. He needs to see them all lined in rows the way he's organized them. It just feels good to know and control one thing in this world. Ambition is another quality some lack, his father says, you have to want more. God helps those who want more. Well, what if most people think more is impossible? Really, why would they consider it?

Meanwhile, it is 1962 or '63, probably August, in our nation's south. From a distance, they are a boat of white faces on a self-contained river, skimming the surface slowly to cause few ripples, needing to think they see clearly and believe what they see. Beneath the water, the owners have designed exotic dioramas of majestic shipwrecks, mermaids, and treasure chests. It is another fabulous world there, just thirty feet down—dazzling, seductive—though completely untouchable.

Hope Against Hope

The butterfly on the teeter totter
The caterpillar on the razor wire
The inchworm on the trip wire
The dung beetle
The corpse fly
The tapeworm
The glow worm on the Christmas tree
The firefly on the electric fence
The fruit fly on the wax fruit
The horse fly on the carousel
The bee on floral wallpaper
Salmon
The mosquito at the blood drive
The moth in the candle factory
The rat in the Cheez Whiz factory
The cat in the Cheez Whiz factory
The giraffe beneath the palm tree
The box turtle in the passing lane
The ant on the Astro turf
The polar bear on its white cement
The goose flock at the fountain pool
The mallard lost among the geese
Truth
Justice
The American Way

Primary Color

Think of it, tens of thousands of years of paintings, if you start with cliffs and caves, that is, and right up to present day, no two have ever been the same. Oh sure, they might belong to the same school or historical moment, but never the same image ever. Even that guy who only painted oranges for his whole career. So it is with people, amazingly enough. They say somewhere in the world is our twin, someone so genetically like us we could be mistaken for them even by family members, but I find it hard to believe. Identical twins are never absolutely alike, their families know who is who, and that's with the same chromosomes. And all this matters, why? Today I am looking at abstract art and thinking how simple primary colors blend to make countless other shades and hues, and how those shades and hues can be applied in so many varied ways, so many different thicknesses, so many different textures, but there is still in all just those primary colors, the essential ground zero. We all have them, these underthings that enjoin us to the groups we're part of, be it species or tribe. Of course, unlike paintings, humans are radically changed by time. Paintings may grow a little less radiant as they age, they may crack a bit. They may suffer at the hands of light. But humans, we really know the difference between being born and having grown old. And we are conscious of it all along the way, that awareness being a condition our animal friends mercifully do not seem to share. Yesterday, my girlfriend's dog died. One day, the old boy is doing well and we're talking hopefully about how much time might be left, then suddenly, within two weeks, he was gone. It happens like that sometimes; something in the body finally gives way, some key system proceeds to fail. But I was talking about paintings, wasn't I, how these I am looking at seem as alive and singular as the day they were finished. Magnificent thing, the making of art. A noble search for accuracy, truth, beauty and meaning within our daily mysteries. Richly undervalued in today's culture, even in rare cases when big investors are involved. But just maybe I have waxed a bit grand. No one ever accused me of being shy about that. In the end, I admit, I am really just worried about my little dog Charlotte, a singular, aged puggle who has gone pure white in the muzzle. One day I may have to put this steadfast friend, as they say, to rest. Do I wish she was a painting? No, she likes to wag her butt too much to make that feasible, so let's not even talk about it. She will die as I will, and we are in a quiet race to see which one lives longest, though secretly, I know the outcome or think I do.

The Song That Never Ends

Wonder of wireless technology,
        this picture frame plays video too,
and here are my children,
        four and six years old,
singing "The Song That Never Ends"
        for exactly 15 seconds.
It barely begins

        before it's over,
which applies too
        to their childhood,
since in the next shot
        they're pushing thirty
and downing Cuervo with friends.

It both amazes and unnerves,
        this post-modern photo magic,
my kids now beaming selfies
        from wherever they choose—
(hang-gliding! rock-climbing!)
        merrily risking perils
I really don't want them to.

And the whole candid mishmash assemblage,
        it loops without end:
one day,
        it is the first of fourth grade
and the next,
        a midriff tattoo!
One second,
        wound in baby blankets,
then voila,
        bound for job interviews!

My mind wheels
with highlights of lives distilled,
Jenga generations
dissembling and restacking,
digital strata
thin as dust on a sill.
My parents, too,
grow aged then regress
before my eyes;
I say my goodbyes
and lo,
here they are, reborn!

It is enough, enough, I say,
this circular pageant
of scene,
this sense of having been,
and been then again!
The dizzying colors
of my daughter's hair—
blond, brunette, pink, green.
My beard whitening
in the time it takes
to squint!

Behold, behold, it says,
what you have lived!
Here you are in Africa
with a machete and no shirt,
did you really have biceps
40 years ago?
And there, there
is sumptuous Melissa,
her youthful breasts

evidenced
          in your mirrored sunglasses. . .
(Ok, that is not on the frame,
          that is more in my head),
but this frame is much like my mind,
          associative and fractured,
given to chaotic forays
          into ardor and pleasure
and guilt and sorrow. . . .

          And then, at last, *fear*.
Of all the issues of aging,
          I dread memory loss most—
what if I don't recognize
          family and friends?
What if I forget
          who I was and am?

On the frame, my uncle frowns
          from his '65 Plymouth.
He doesn't give two hoots
          what we remember or don't,
and for a moment I wish
          I was equally cynical.

But then, right on cue,
          my kids are singing again,
providing a kind of closure,
          this theoretically should lack,
and transforming me
          once more
into a young father at bath-time
          with another chance
to tuck them in.
          Lucky me. Lucky me.
I'll take it
          before it's gone.

Wonder Bread

Lately, I meet mornings unsure of what to do with myself. I can either go to my desk or not; it doesn't really matter. It's not like when something really had to happen, no matter what. The kids needed to be at school on time, lunches must get made, the world would tilt if I turned my head even a moment. I miss assembling those lunches: the baggies of carrot sticks and apple slices, the pudding cups, sandwiches stamped in circles (only creamy! no crust!) and those colorful, cartoon lunch boxes by which they made themselves known—Ninja Turtles, Buzz Lightyear, Miss Kitty, Shrek. My children are grown. When I meet them for dinner, they clean their plates without having to be told. Sometimes they even pick up the check, leaving tips I am proud of, before looking both ways and easing safely out of the parking lot back into their lives. While I, I return here, to wake in the morning with my faithful dog and think shall I go to my desk or not? A few more words in me or not? It all really seemed to matter once, not long ago, and I'm glad it did. I wouldn't change much. Truly, what I fear most about aging is dementia, not remembering my kids. I watched a movie the other day starring Rita Hayworth. Known as "The Love Goddess," the most popular pinup girl of World War II, she, not Ginger Rogers, was Fred Astaire's favorite dance partner. And she died in her sixties unable to remember any of it. Her costar, though this is another story, never got another good part. He passed in his mere fifties—just drank himself to death. Stardom is hard on people. Give me the simple life. If I do get Alzheimer's, let me get stuck reliving those mornings making lunches. The same thing over and over again. Everybody late, rushing around, cramming stuff into bookbags, and scurrying out to the car. Then piling in together. Just being there, buckled in next to each other, sitting in line, waiting to drop off at the front doors. I could wait like that. I could wait like that for as long as it takes.

Acknowledgments

The author wishes to thank the editors of the following venues in which these poems first appeared:

32 Poems, "The Dance," "Shelter"

Brevity, "True North"

The Café Review, "Song for the Outer Doors"

Chautauqua Review, "Happy Hour at the House of Tang"

The Connecticut River Review, "Music Box"

The James Dickey Review, "Gasoline," "Grocery List," "Poses, Colorado 1964," "Sunning"

The Greensboro Review, "Knowing"

New Ohio Review, "Blink Once for Yes"

Poetry Miscellany, "In Media Res" (as "Portrait"), "Shroud," and "The Song That Never Ends"

Salt, "Short Cake," "Wonder Bread"

You Are the River, Literature Inspired by the North Carolina Museum of Art, ed., Helena Feder, "Hand"

Special thanks to Cynthia Huntington for her help with this manuscript.

MARK COX has authored six other volumes of poetry, the most recent being *Readiness* (2018) and *Sorrow Bread: Poems* 1984-2015 (2017). He has a forty-year history of publication in prominent magazines and his honors include a Whiting Writers' Award, a Pushcart Prize, the Oklahoma Book Award, and The Society of Midland Authors Poetry Prize. He chairs the Department of Creative Writing at UNC Wilmington and teaches in the Vermont College of Fine Arts MFA Program.

www.ingramcontent.com/pod-product-compliance
Lightning Source LLC
LaVergne TN
LVHW051015080826
845145LV00009B/2636

* 9 7 8 1 9 5 0 4 1 3 7 9 9 *